Berklee Jazz Bass

To access audio visit:
www.halleonard.com/mylibrary

"Enter Code"
7287-4273-0668-4960

RICH APPLEMAN
WHIT BROWNE
BRUCE GERTZ

MUSICIANS

Bass: Rich Appleman, Whit Browne, Bruce Gertz

Drums: Austin McMahon

Guitar: Larry Baione

Piano: Tim Ray

BERKLEE PRESS

Editor in Chief: Jonathan Feist
Senior Vice President of Online Learning and Continuing Education/CEO of Berklee Online: Debbie Cavalier
Assistant Vice President of Marketing and Recruitment for Berklee Online: Mike King
Dean of Continuing Education: Carin Nuernberg
Editorial Assistants: Matthew Dunkel, Reilly Garrett, Emily Jones, Eloise Kelsey, Zoë Lustri, Sarah Walk
Photo of Rich Appleman by Moti Hodis (www.motihodisphotography.com)
Photo of Whit Browne by Rich Appleman
Photo of Bruce Gertz by Eva Gertz
Bass fingering photos by Jonathan Feist
Cover Designer: Tim Scholl and Small Mammoth Design

ISBN 978-0-87639-169-3

online.berklee.edu

DISTRIBUTED BY

HAL•LEONARD®
CORPORATION
7777 W. BLUEMOUND RD. P.O. BOX 13819
MILWAUKEE, WISCONSIN 53213

1140 Boylston Street
Boston, MA 02215-3693 USA
(617) 747-2146

Visit Berklee Press Online at
www.berkleepress.com

Visit Hal Leonard Online
www.halleonard.com

Berklee Press, a publishing activity of Berklee College of Music, is a not-for-profit educational publisher.
Available proceeds from the sales of our products are contributed to the scholarship funds of the college.

CONTENTS

PREFACE

This book will help you to learn the "language" of jazz bass playing, whether you are a jazz novice or a more experienced player, hoping to improve your jazz acumen. It is aimed at bassists who are comfortable with the fundamentals and geography of the bass.

This is not a method book for learning fingerings and positions. Rather, it will help you to use those rudiments to create interesting and motivating bass lines and melodically interesting solos.

You may notice some variations between the audio tracks and provided notation, with slightly different rhythmic interpretations and pitch choices. This spirit of interpretation is common in how jazz musicians use written notation—as long as you keep the time and stay true to the harmonic context.

We hope that this book will help you become a valuable asset to any jazz group.

—The Authors

ACCESSING THE AUDIO

To access the accompanying audio, go to www.halleonard.com/mylibrary and enter the code found on the first page of this book. This code will grant you instant access to every example. Examples with accompanying audio are marked with an audio icon.

CHAPTER 1

Developing Your Jazz Bass Concept

When developing your "concept" or idea of jazz bass playing, the four T's can be helpful: time, tonality, timbre, and taste. These are the most important components for a strong, supportive bass line.

- **Time:** All jazz music has a time concept: fast, slow, swing, broken, straight eighths, free, etc. Additionally, bass line shapes are generally constructed by following the music's phrase structure, usually four-bar phrases. In 4/4 time, the beat 4 to beat 1 resolution is very strong/important, so keep the 4-to-1 concepts (discussed in this chapter) in mind.

- **Tonality:** In the overtone series, the strongest notes sounding over the fundamental are the octave, 5, octave, and 3. So, the root and 5 of any chord or tonality are the most stable and supportive notes. Always be aware of how your notes sound or are functioning in a harmonic context. Root, 5, approach, tension, etc.

- **Timbre:** Your sound. Listen closely to the "masters," your favorites, and yourself.

- **Taste:** How you use the above. To develop your sense of taste, steal/borrow bass line ideas from your favorite players, and make them your own.

Our function or "job" as bassists is to provide the beat and ground the harmony. Forward motion and resolution of both harmony and rhythm provide a direction that supports the melody and/or improvisation. This role of support is what we call "bass bass." We want the other musicians in the group to know where we are going before we get there. We want them to hear the chord progressions through our choice of notes in the bass line.

Here's a lead sheet performed by the three authors, each using their own concept: first Rich, then Whit, then Bruce. Check it out! We will be discussing the techniques we use here throughout the book.

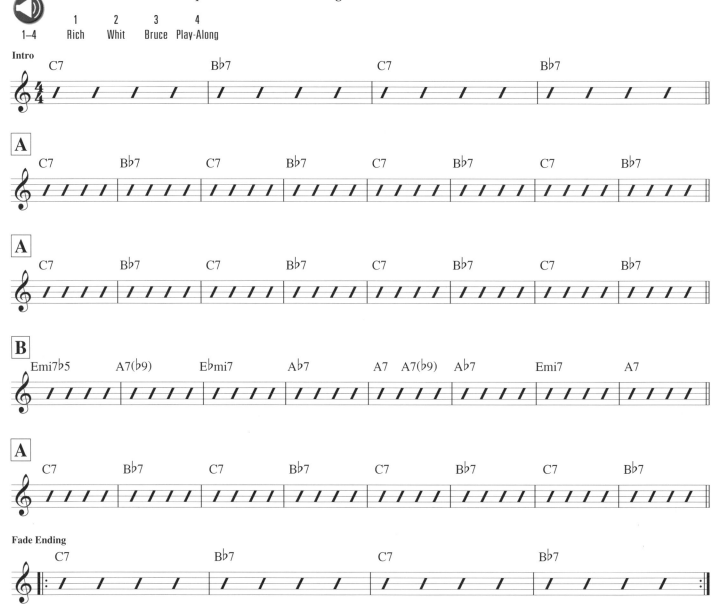

FIG. 1.1. Introductory Etude

THE 4-TO-1 CONCEPT

The concept of *4 to 1* is that the fourth beat of a bar sets up the downbeat of the next bar—both rhythmically and harmonically.

FIG. 1.2. 4-to-1 Concept: Beats

Similarly, the fourth bar of a phrase sets up the downbeat of the next phrase.

FIG. 1.3. 4-to-1 Concept: Phrases

In either case, going from the 4 to the 1 creates a sense of forward motion. Every note you play has to swing. Each note has a purpose, or "function," while serving as a stepping-stone to the next note, whether it is within the same chord or resolving to a new chord. Examples in chapter 2 ("Building Bass Lines") demonstrate these concepts.

NOTE RESOLUTION

Note resolutions in jazz bass lines generally come from cycle-V bass motion, a series of fifths as shown by the "circle of fifths."

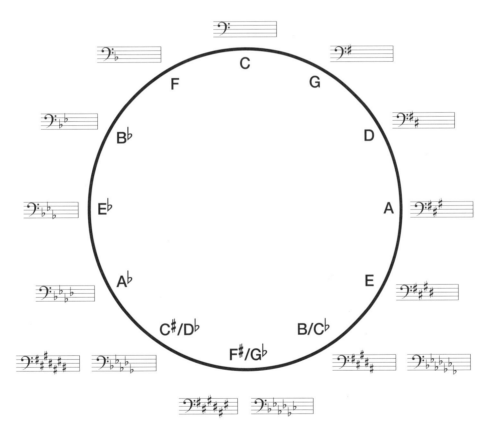

FIG. 1.4. Circle of Fifths

Many jazz resolutions come from this cycle, such as IImi7 to V7 to I (e.g., Dmi7 G7 C).

Bass line note resolutions are strongest when the notes "lead" or "resolve" by either the 5, by half step "chromatic passing tones" (see chapter 3), or by scale step of the key.

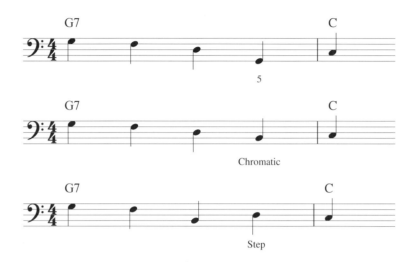

FIG. 1.5. Bass Line Resolutions

FINAL THOUGHTS

The included play-along audio is a good place to start when working with this book. Many of the chord progressions we use here can also be found on recordings of famous masters such as Miles Davis, Herbie Hancock, John Coltrane, Dizzy Gillespie, Charlie Parker, and many others. Throughout the book, we suggest some classic jazz recordings for you to practice with.

Your "concept" is your unique set of ideas about how to construct your part. Developing one's concept is not something that many musicians work on in the abstract. However, as you work on particular tunes and think about your sense of time for it, the tonality, the timbre/sound quality, and its speed or register, your overall concept of playing the bass will develop.

There are certain basics you have to cover, but also a lot of possible variation in how you color it. Like, if you make a pizza, you have to have the dough. But the sauce and toppings can vary, and those will define what kind of pizza you're making. Playing bass is the same.

There's a reason why certain bass players' phones ring and others don't. A big part of that is their concept: how they approach constructing their parts. You also have to match your overall approach to the specific tunes you play. Some concepts will work well for blues, others for faster Latin styles.

It's just important to have an idea. Your concept will come to include everything about your playing, from the choice of notes to the sound on the amp/strings to the range that you tend to play in. Being aware of these elements is important to developing your idea of how you are going to play jazz bass lines.

CHAPTER 2

Building Bass Lines

Bass players are like architects. We design lines that create a strong foundation that must support the rest of the music. While we sometimes also play solos, our primary job is in creating that foundation.

There are two primary components of a jazz bass line: notes and rhythms.

CHOOSING NOTES

Chord symbols on a lead sheet show you which notes to use for constructing your lines. Your notes can be drawn from the chord tones, or as we'll see in chapter 3, from the key and other sources.

A chord symbol consists of a letter, indicating the root, an abbreviation describing the quality of the triad, the seventh, and possibly a tension up above that. The numbers refer to scale tones, with the root being 1, the 5 for the fifth note of the scale, and so on. The placement of the symbol shows the harmonic rhythm of the tune—how long that chord stays in effect. The chord lasts until the symbol changes to a new chord symbol, hence the term "chord changes."

FIG. 2.1. Chord and Scale Degrees for C Major

Here are the diatonic chords for the key of C major—the chords possible to create using the notes from the C major scale.

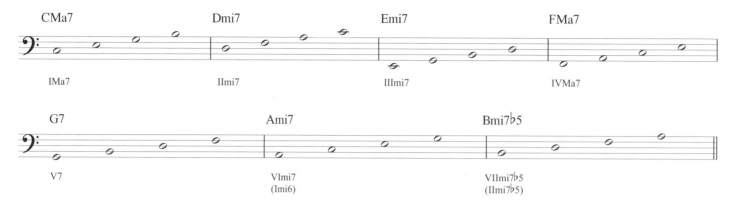

FIG. 2.2. Diatonic Chords and Modes of C Major

When you develop your bass lines, chord tones are one of the primary sources of notes. We will look at other sources throughout this book. But to summarize, they come primarily from three sources:

- chord tones (R 3 5 7)
- scale tones
- the notes "between" the chord tones and scale tones (e.g., passing tones, chromatic approach tones, etc.)

CHORD SYMBOLS

Chords are specified in lead sheet notation with chord symbols. Figure 2.3 shows the common chord suffix symbols in the key of C and some of the standard abbreviations you will find for them (which will vary across regions, styles, and publishers). Also listed are the notes of that chord, with C as the root.

Quality	Abbreviations	Examples	Notes for C Root (Bottom to Top)
Major	(none, triad only)	C	C E G
	Ma, Maj, M, △	CMa7	C E G B
Minor	mi, min, m, –	Cmi, or C–	C E♭ G
Suspended 2 (often referred to as 9)	sus2	Csus2	C D G
Suspended 4	sus4, sus	Csus4	C F G
Diminished	dim, ᵒ	Cdim	C E♭ G♭
Augmented	aug, +	Caug	C E G♯
Five	5	C5	C G
Sixth	6	C6	C E G A
		C–6	C E♭ G A
Seventh	7	CMaj7	C E G B
		C7	C E G B♭
		C7♭5	C E G♭ B♭
		Caug7	C E G♯ B♭
		C–7	C E♭ G B♭
		C–(Maj7)	C E♭ G B
		Cdim7	C E♭ G♭ B♭♭
		Cdim(Maj7)	C E♭ G♭ B
		C7sus4	C F G B♭
Half Diminished	mi7♭5, –7♭5, ø	C–7♭5	C E♭ G♭ B♭
Tensions	♭9, 9, ♯9, 10, 11, ♯11, ♭13, 13	Note: Usage is subject to context. Not all tensions are available on all chords. C7(9,♯11,13)	C E G B♭ D F♯ A
Chord with Designated Bass Note	/	C/D	D C E G

FIG. 2.3. Common Chord Symbols

BASS LINES FROM CHORD SCALES

Chords have associated *chord scales*—the scales comprised of the notes associated with that chord in its current context, including tensions, which when set between the chord tones, act as passing tones.

For example, Mixolydian is a chord scale of a dominant seventh chord. It is a mode of the major scale. Here is F Mixolydian, shown as an ascending chord scale and as an arpeggio.

FIG. 2.4. Mixolydian

Here's another chord scale that could go with F7: F Lydian ♭7.

FIG. 2.5. Lydian ♭7

These scales are important sources of notes for both creating bass lines and for soloing.

Chords and Modes

Modes are a way to define the tonality. When you're building a bass line, you can use the mode associated with the current chord as a source for your notes.

The basic seven modes are essentially displaced major scales. The current chord's root gives you the starting note of the mode. The other notes come from the tune's key, or perhaps the melody. Modes always have one note of every letter. This therefore changes the pattern of half steps and whole steps of the scale at the root of the key. The mode then reinforces the current chord's function within the chord progression.

To find the mode associated with the current chord, you need to understand how that chord is used, in the context, and listen. Look to the key signature and then to the melody, and fill in the scale based on the chord's root (sometimes referenced as a Roman numeral indicating the chord's function, such as I VI II V) using the diatonic notes of its key and melodic context, to arrive at the mode. This association is also called the "chord scale" of a chord.

For a basic understanding of chord scale theory, begin with the seven modes of the major scale. There are many other possibilities, but these are a good place to start.

This chart shows the modes associated with the chords diatonic to C major. If the melody happens to have non-diatonic notes, that could change the best mode for that chord.

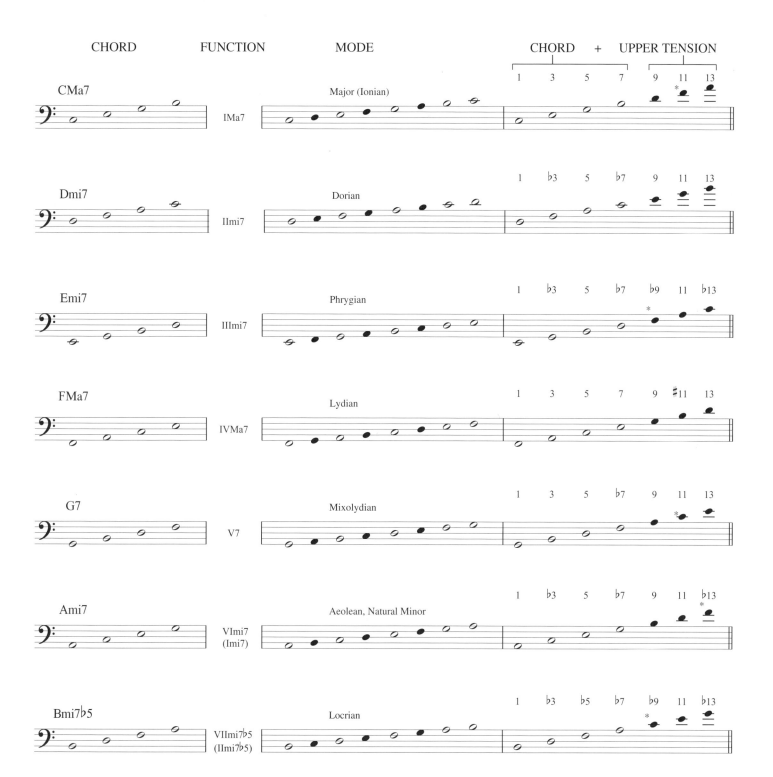

* Indicates a note that should resolve, often called an "avoid note"

FIG. 2.6. Modes

Practicing Modes

In this exercise, the same D minor chord is set in the context of different keys. Notice how the line changes to accommodate the different key signatures—especially how the same D minor chord functions in each of these examples, with the mode's half steps defining the key. The downbeats here are not always the root; the 3 or 5 is sometimes on the downbeat instead.

FIG. 2.7. Mode Practice

RHYTHMIC FEEL

The second dimension of a bass line is the rhythm, and that begins with determining how many notes you will play per measure. One of our jobs as bass players is to keep time. In addition, you are the architect of the music's foundation. So, how you use the notes in a time feel is very important.

Each musical style calls for a certain rhythmic approach or "feel." Latin and rock music are mostly even eighth notes, while jazz swing is more like eighth-note triplets. Other styles may use combinations of swing and even eighth notes or sixteenth notes.

Some players have natural rhythm and time feel, while others need to develop it more. Being a musician with a good time feel is an excellent goal on any instrument. First, be aware of your internal clock (heartbeat). Most of us have a heartbeat of 60 to 100 beats per minute (bpm), depending on our activity level (running at 100 bpm, walking at 80 bpm, or sleeping at 60 bpm). The average pulse when playing music is usually somewhere between 72 and 100 bpm. For this reason, we feel time most comfortably when we can relate it to that range of pulse.

Fast tempos (144 to 400 bpm) feel more comfortable when cut in half—72 to 200 bpm, felt in half notes rather than quarter notes. Many people say, the faster the tempo, the slower you beat your foot. Slow tempos (40 to 72 bpm) feel more comfortable when doubled (80 to 144 bpm). So, you might be feeling a different subdivision or multiple of the tempo you are actually performing.

Practicing with a metronome, sequencer, or drum machine will help supply a good reference. However, to get a good "time feel," it is necessary to interact with other musicians, and listen. Practice along with recordings while paying close attention to the drums and bass, and try to lock in with the rhythm section so that you feel like part of the groove. Notice how the music feels better when you play the time a certain way: the length of your notes, the space between them, and whether they are more aggressive (on top of the beat), less aggressive (in the middle of the beat), or relaxed (on the back of the beat).

Styles and grooves are best learned with recordings and live bands rather than just a metronome or other mechanical time reference. Authentic grooves for different styles involve subtle approaches to dynamics and articulation. It takes years to master the idioms of jazz, Latin, funk, and classical music. When you have a strong time feel, other players can and do rely on your bass alone. In a duo with bass and another instrument, we are depended upon to supply the groove and the chord changes without a drummer.

In jazz, a bass player must be able to provide a solid two feel and a solid 4/4 walking feel. *Walking* means playing four quarter notes per bar, but moving with forward motion. Most of the time, this movement is in the context of a chord progression. You must be able to provide a walking feel that moves and progresses. The two feel is more stable, using the roots and 5's, which are the most stable notes in the overtone series.

The "Two" Feel

A *two feel* has two half notes per measure in 4/4 (or "common") time. This feel was very common in early jazz, where it was often played by the piano player's left hand, the tuba, or the acoustic bass (with fingers/pizzicato or bow/ arco). The two feel is still used and can be the perfect way to lay down a solid, danceable groove that outlines the harmony. Keeping the two feel sound in your head while playing either a walking bass line or a solo is a great way to keep your place in the form of a tune.

Take some time to listen to great jazz bassists play two-feel bass lines, such as Ray Brown, Ron Carter, Paul Chambers, Slam Stewart, and Christian McBride. How you play this feel is an important part of your bass personality.

"Fall Foliage" in Two Keys

Using roots and 5's on this chord progression gives us a solid two feel. "Fall Foliage" is played here with a two feel. It uses cycle-V bass motion. First listen to the full band track, and then play along with the recording. Try it in these two different keys: E minor (good for guitarists) and D minor (also good for horn players). Be aware of the form and how each section is slightly different.

On the recording, we play it twice, the second time as double time. Listen to the countoff.

5   6
Full Band   Play-Along

FIG. 2.8. "Fall Foliage" in E Minor

When you listen to this track in D minor, notice the length of the bass player's half notes. Again, we play it double time, the second time through.

7   8
Full Band Play-Along

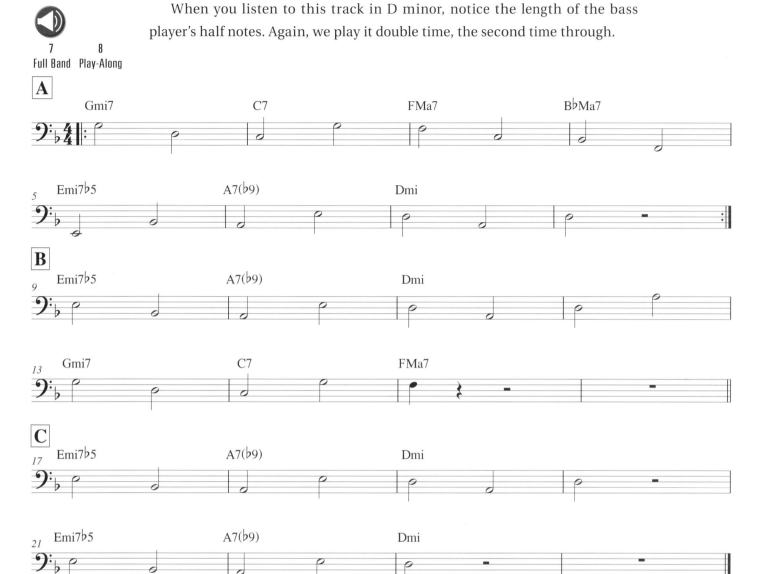

FIG. 2.9. "Fall Foliage" in D Minor

"Take a Subway"

Roots and 5's also work on this tune. It is fine to occasionally use some quarter notes in a two feel.

Notice that the harmonic rhythm in "Fall Foliage" is one chord per measure. On this tune, the harmonic rhythm is more sparse and often varies. Harmonic rhythm will inform your time and tonality concepts. When chords move faster, they will give you more ideas for constructing your lines. A slower harmonic rhythm requires more thought to construct an interesting line.

When you practice "Take a Subway," memorize this ending. It is widely used.

9   10
Full Band   Play-Along

FIG. 2.10. "Take a Subway"

"Quiet as the Early Light"

11   12
Full Band Play-Along

Notice that this two feel uses notes other than roots and 5's. It is also a good example of a minor tonality in the A section and its relative major in the B section: C minor to E♭ major.

FIG. 2.11. "Quiet as the Early Light"

"Island of Tom"

13   14
Full Band   Play-Along

Notice the length of the notes in this calypso tune. You can add personality and spice by the length and rhythm.

Calypso

FIG. 2.12. "Island of Tom"

"Apple Honey"

In addition to the notes and the rhythm, be aware of the shape of your lines.

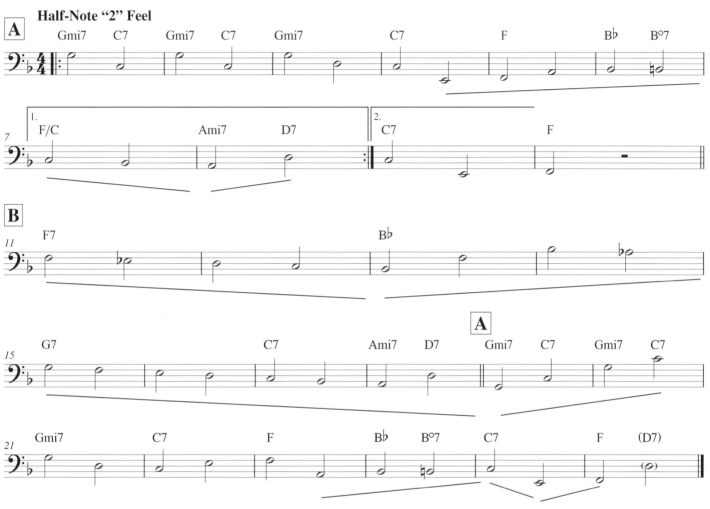

FIG. 2.13. "Apple Honey"

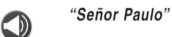

"Señor Paulo"

A famous minor blues progression.

FIG. 2.14. "Señor Paulo"

Four Feel and Walking Bass

A four-feel has a quarter note on every beat of 4/4 time. Depending on style and tempo, playing just chord roots can work, for a 4/4 line.

Figure 2.15 shows four-feel lines, both with one chord per measure and with two chords per measure. These simple lines just play the chord roots. They ground the harmonies, but there is not a sense of motion or shape to the lines.

FIG. 2.15. Four-Feel Bass Lines

One of the early styles that featured this type of bass line is Kansas City swing, with Pops Foster playing four quarter notes per bar; he is considered the father of walking bass. Pops moved from a half-note feel to a quarter-note feel. It caught on in the 1930s and '40s, and people liked dancing to it.

A *walking bass line* is a 4/4 line that has melodic direction, rather than staying on just the root, or on the root and 5.

Some may think that playing walking bass is easy, but it is actually quite a challenge to come up with lines that work with the chord changes and use the quarter-note rhythm. You can use shapes to create dynamics and climaxes. It's a lot of fun!

Rhythm Changes: Mixing Two and Four Feel

It's very common to start a tune in a two feel and move into a four feel. Here's an example, using rhythm changes—one of the most popular jazz progressions, most famously used in Gershwin's "I Got Rhythm."

In early jazz, it was common to use a two feel in the bass part, a practice derived from ragtime piano players' left-hand lines, and perhaps tuba lines.

In the 1930s, as the music moved into the swing period, the 4/4 walking bass became more popular, but often, the two feels were mixed. In rhythm changes, for example, it is common to play the first two A sections in a two feel and then move to a four feel at the bridge.

Staying in two can really build excitement and tension, which gets released when it moves to four. Ray Brown was famous for prolonging the two to build extra tension.

The way you determine what octave to play in can have an effect on the music. Experienced bass players are very aware of the range of their lines. Sometimes, making large jumps look like they would sound awkward, but they might actually be effective shapes. In figure 2.16, notice bar 2 versus bar 4, where the line first goes down and then goes up to the higher F. Changing the 2-bar phrases adds variation to the line.

19   20
Full Band Play-Along

FIG. 2.16. Rhythm Changes, Mixing Two Feel and Walking Bass

This bass line on rhythm changes is a good example of using modes. Where there are non-diatonic chords, such as bars 5 and 6, this line sticks to chord tones.

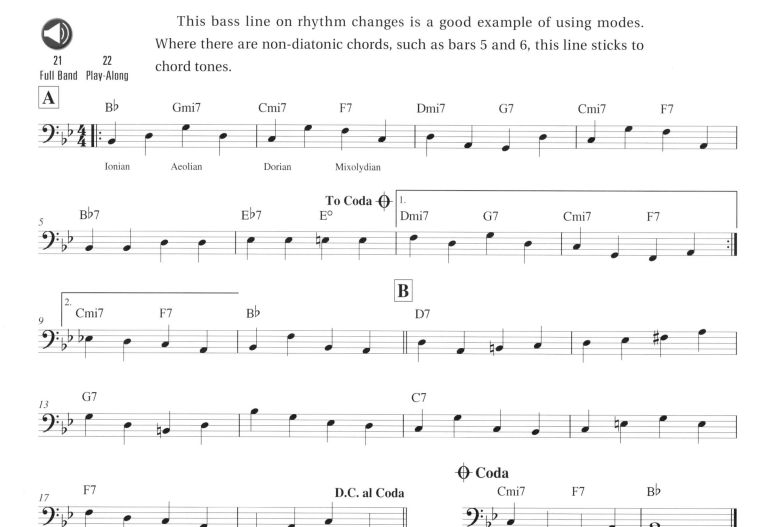

FIG. 2.17. Rhythm Changes: Roots and 5's

This rhythm changes exercise is a good one for working on for both right- and left-hand articulation. Try it at different speeds with a metronome on 2 and 4.

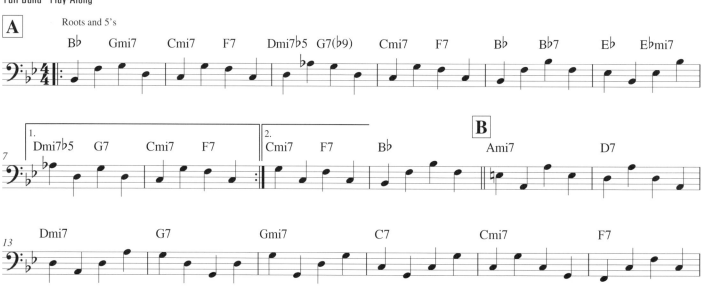

FIG. 2.18. Rhythm Changes: Roots and 5's

"Spare Apple Parts"

The bass line at the B section of "Spare Apple Parts" is a good example of using modes. Where there are non-diatonic chords, such as the C7(♭9) in bar 4 (A section), the line uses chromatic approach tones, rather than a mode.

25 26
Full Band   Play-Along

FIG. 2.19. "Spare Apple Parts"

Cycle V Practice

This series of exercises is based on the cycle of fifths, ascending, arpeggiating each chord. Also try it descending.

FIG. 2.20. Root Position Chord Arpeggios

27 28
Full Band Play-Along

Consider inversions. Starting on a chord tone other than the root can make your line more melodic. On the recording, the second time through, we play it double time.

FIG. 2.21. Cycle V Arpeggios and Inversions

II V'S

These exercises are based on II V's: a minor II chord and a V, which also moves in cycle-V bass motion. You can apply modal concept to these II V's using a Dorian mode on the II chord and a Mixolydian mode on the V chord. Realize that each II V introduces a new key.

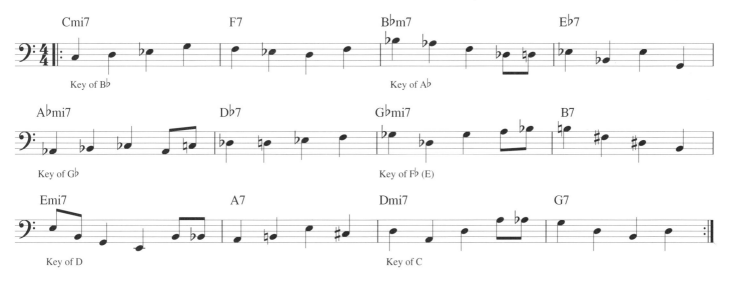

FIG. 2.22. Cycle V Example 1

FIG. 2.23. Cycle V Example 2

We want to think enharmonically when in actual performance. F♭ = E and C♭ = B because they are faster to think, hear, and communicate.

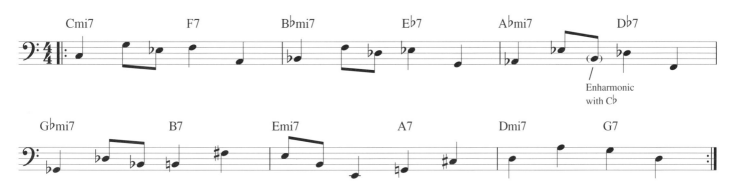

FIG. 2.24. Cycle V Example 3

CHAPTER 3

The Notes Between the Notes

The notes between the notes give your bass line the movement it needs to walk. They are usually scalar or chromatic notes (above or below), and they can be used in many different ways. *Scalar* notes (S in analysis) are drawn from the diatonic scale, such as a D to E on a CMa7 chord. *Chromatic* notes (CH in analysis) move into the chord tone by half step, such as D♯ to E. Because the half step is the smallest interval in our equal temperament system, the use of chromatic passing notes into chord tones is a good way to give your lines both direction and spice.

If it moves up to the chord tone, it is said to be "ascending;" if down, it is "descending." A *double chromatic approach* (Dbl. CH) is two notes sequentially before the chord tone.

An *indirect resolution* (I.R.) is approaching a chord tone from both above and below.

FIG. 3.1. Non-Chord Tones

Figure 3.2 shows a C major triad (1, 3, 5) with the note D (the 2 of the C major scale, abbreviated S2) functioning as a scale approach to E, the third of the chord. The resulting bass line (1, 2, 3, 5) is very common. It can be used again on the F chord (F, A, C, being the F major triad and G being S2).

FIG. 3.2. R S2 3 5 Lines

As the above examples and figure 3.3 illustrate, approach notes generally should occur on beats 2 and 4, allowing for the roots and chord tones to occur on beats 1 and 3.

Walking bass lines imply movement. The best lines, like a great sauce, have a combination of stable chord sound and flavorful approach notes.

SCALAR BASS LINES

Figure 3.3 shows a scale passing line in cycle V motion over the first eight measures of a popular standard progression. Notice that when the chords move down a perfect fifth, the scale brings you directly to the next root over four beats. These notes give you a walking feel and also a melodic shape.

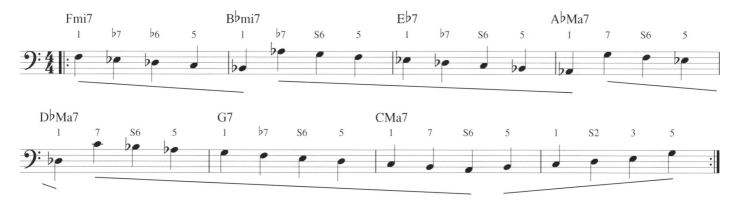

FIG. 3.3. Scalar Bass Line

CHROMATIC PASSING TONES

Chromatic passing tones will always be a half step approaching the chord tones R 3 5 7. The most common approaches are:

- from below or above
- a combination of above/below and below/above
- double chromatic from above
- double chromatic from below

If something sounds funny, you're probably just a half step away from a good note!

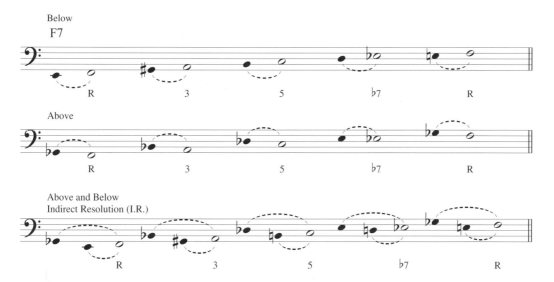

FIG. 3.4. Chromatic Passing Tones

Here are some examples of using scale and chromatic passing tones from below and above (also called "double chromatic approach").

FIG. 3.5. Double Chromatic Approach

It is important that the passing tones lead to a chord tone placed on the strong beats, or "1" and "3," of the measure. These passing tones can indicate a displaced chord tone to the weak beats "2" and "4," but that is a more advanced concept that we will illustrate later.

29   30
Full Band   Play-Along

Figure 3.6 uses passing tones on a common 12-bar blues progression. Here, the chord root always sounds at the chord change. Some notes, such as the C in bar 2 beat 4, can be analyzed in multiple ways (here, as S2 or a 9).

FIG. 3.6. 12-Bar Blues Example 1

31   32
Full Band Play-Along

In this example, notice that on measures 7 and 11, we use a note other than the root when the chord changes.

FIG. 3.7. 12-Bar Blues Example 2

BLUES WITH SCALE AND CHROMATIC APPROACH NOTES

Practice these progressions. Note the shape of the line, and identify which notes are chord tones and which are approach notes.

Approach-Note Practice 1

Every now and then, making a leap is a good way to catch people's ears. Here, notice the leaps in bar 4 (beats 3 to 4), bar 6 (beats 1 to 2), and bar 11 (beats 1 to 2). Consider the melodic shape of your bass line (drawn in, on figure 3.8).

FIG. 3.8. Approach-Note Practice 1

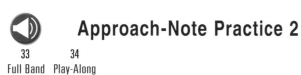

Approach-Note Practice 2

33   34
Full Band   Play-Along

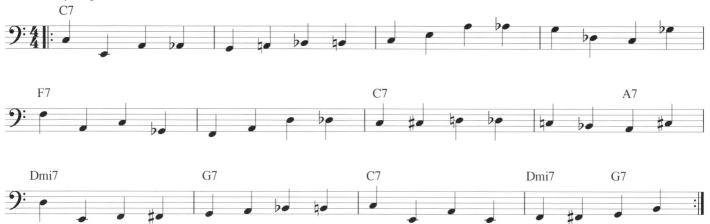

FIG. 3.9. Approach-Note Practice 2

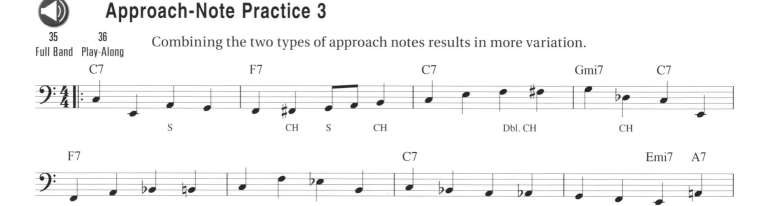

Approach-Note Practice 3

35   36
Full Band   Play-Along

Combining the two types of approach notes results in more variation.

FIG. 3.10. Approach-Note Practice 3

Approach-Note Practice 4

37   38
Full Band   Play-Along

FIG. 3.11. Approach-Note Practice 4

Approach-Note Practice 5

39
Full Band

40
Play-Along

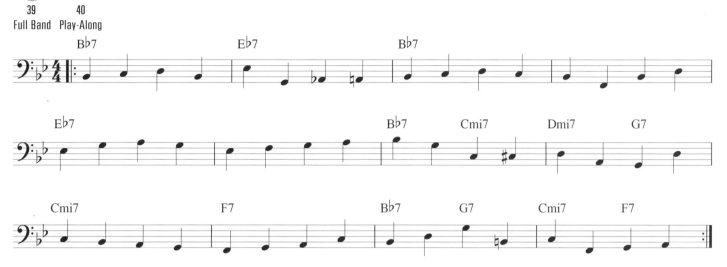

FIG. **3.12.** Approach-Note Practice 5: Blues in B♭

Approach-Note Practice 6

41
Full Band

42
Play-Along

FIG. **3.13.** Approach-Note Practice 6: Blues in G

CYCLE V PRACTICE

This series of exercises is based on the cycle of fifths, similar to those in chapter 2. Here, some scale approach notes have been added. Parentheses ( ) indicate approach notes between chord tones.

In bar 9, within the chord, the 2 (F♯) is actually the V (F♯) of the V (B), so the cycle of fifths exists within the chord as well.

FIG. 3.14. Cycle V Exercise with Passing Tones

Strive to make the line resolve scale tone, chromatic tone, etc., within the chord. Think about the weight and length of your notes.

Note that the scale approach notes can move by whole step/half step, in addition to a fifth or fourth interval, which creates a V to I sound. Always be aware of where you have been and where you are going.

FIG. 3.15. Cycle V Exercise with Approach Notes 1

47   48
Full Band   Play-Along

Here's a nicely shaped bass line using II V's in cycle V.

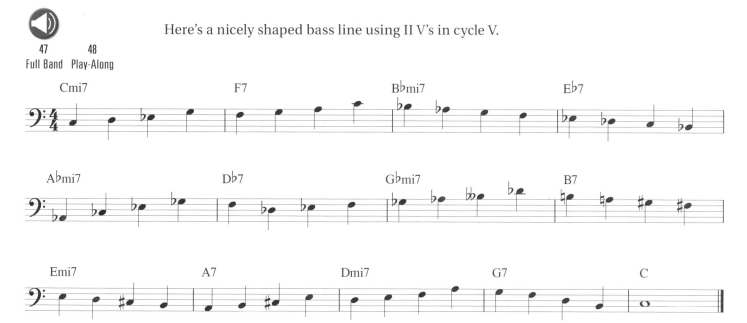

FIG. 3.16. Cycle V Exercise with Approach Notes 2

49   50
Full Band   Play-Along

This line adds some II V's and a little rhythmic spice. Notice the added swing eighth notes and the different harmonic rhythm.

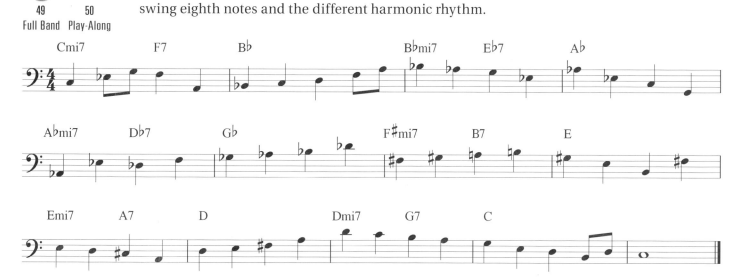

FIG. 3.17. Combination Scale Arpeggios

COMMON CHORD TONE APPROACHES

Here are three common C chords followed by a chart of possible approaches into their chord tones.

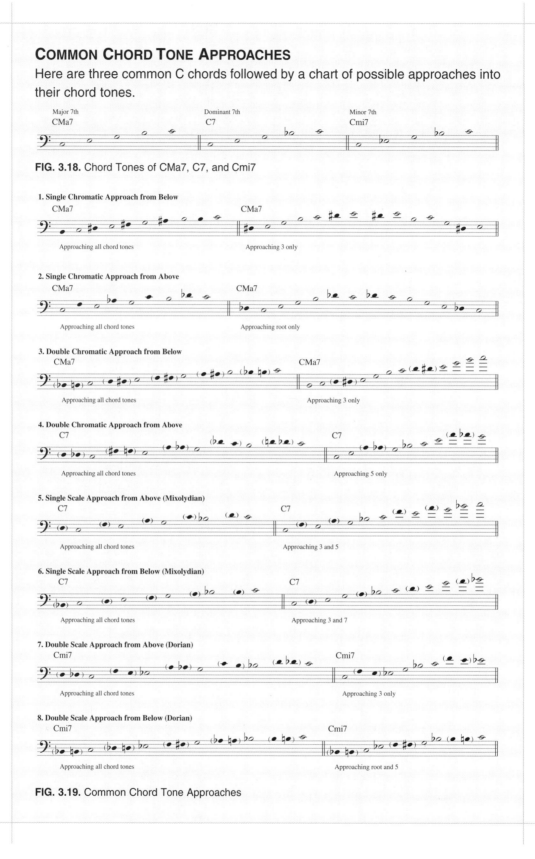

FIG. 3.18. Chord Tones of CMa7, C7, and Cmi7

FIG. 3.19. Common Chord Tone Approaches

Chord Progressions and Walking Bass

Chord progressions influence walking lines.

II V BLUES

The following exercises are based on a famous progression from the bebop period. Adding chords can also give motion and interest to your line. The chord pair IImi7 V7 is a particularly common way to increase harmonic interest. This type of reharmonization was widely used in bebop.

The addition of chords to a progression can be both challenging and helpful. The chords give you a really good idea of what to play. At the same time, they make you responsible for providing the bass function.

Practice the exercises, and notice how the substitute chords and approach notes add interest and shape to the bass lines.

"Alice in Azure"

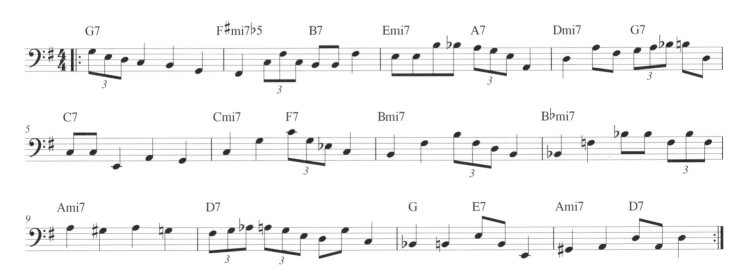

FIG. 4.1. "Alice in Azure"

"Cobalt Alicia"

An x notehead (✕) means a dead, ghost, or muted note—a note that makes an unpitched, percussive sound, rather than sounding a note. To deaden a string, hold it still with the left hand, but don't push the string all the way down to the fingerboard. The dead note could be on the same string or on an adjacent string to the preceding note. Bar 9 has a *rake*, which is a series of dead notes across several strings. For more about articulations, see chapter 5.

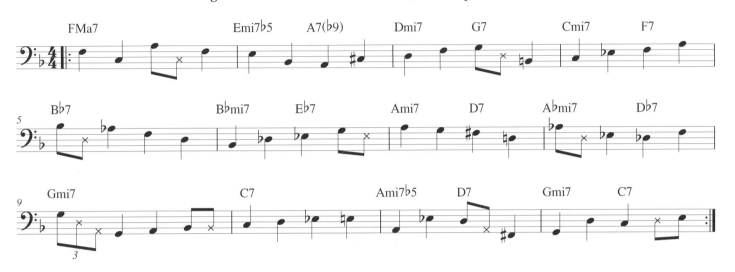

FIG. 4.2. "Cobalt Alicia"

SubV7

A substitute V7 (subV7) is a chord that uses the same tritone (3 and 7) as the V7 but gives you chromatic bass motion instead of cycle-V bass motion.

In bar 3 to 4, notice that the E♭7 and D♭7 create chromatic bass motion. The tritone (3 and 7) of E♭7 is the same tritone as in A7. It gives you the chromatic bass motion, but retains the original tritone of the V7. This tritone's instability creates a dominant sound.

FIG. 4.3. Substitute Chords

"Alice in Blueland"

51   52
Full Band Play-Along

"Alice in Blueland" features chords using octave jumps in a chromatic descending line (substitute dominant chords).

FIG. 4.4. "Alice in Blueland"

POST-BOP

Here are two examples of familiar post-bop progressions. Post bop has a harder sound, with forms that were more original, rather than being based on standard tunes. Bebop was characterized by taking standard chord progressions (e.g., "I Got Rhythm," "Honeysuckle Rose," "All the Things You Are"), and sometimes reharmonizing them and mixing them together. Post-bop musicians were more into writing their own tunes and being more adventurous, stretching the harmonies. "Giant Steps" was a famous post-bop tune by John Coltrane. He actually got the idea for the progression (with three tonal centers) from a famous theory book by Nicolas Slominsky. After post-bop, jazz then moved into the modal and free jazz periods of John Coltrane, Ornette Coleman, Charles Mingus, and Miles Davis.

"Big Shoes"

53   54
Full Band Play-Along

This is a great progression to memorize. It is usually played fast, but it also works as a ballad or bossa nova.

Chorus 1

FIG. 4.5. "Big Shoes"

"Giant Loops"

This is an exercise in both ear training and walking bass, over a popular *three-tonic cycle* chord progression (three keys a major third apart). Listen to the example in track 55, noting how the bass line connects the chords. Then practice creating a similar type of line against track 56.

55   56
Full Band Play-Along

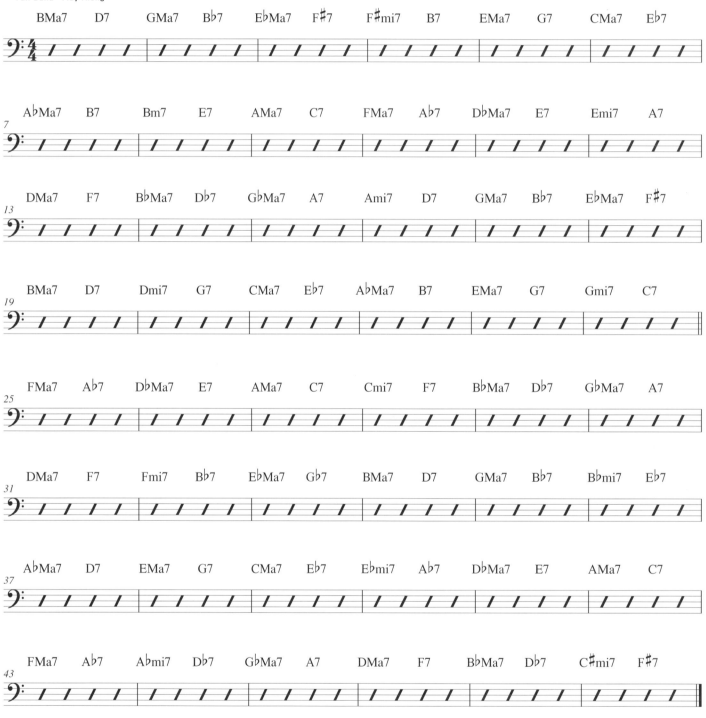

FIG. 4.6. "Giant Loops"

"Isotoner"

57   58
Full Band Play-Along

This is another popular post-bop progression—a post-bop interpretation of the blues. It starts out sounding like a regular 12-bar blues, but then uses a series of sus4 chords, starting in bar 6.

FIG. 4.7. "Isotoner"

DISPLACING THE ROOT

In general, it is safest to always play the root on the first beat, and in jazz, most people want to hear that. But here are some other possibilities.

59   60
Full Band Play-Along

At bar 10, notice that the chord starts on the 3rd on beat 1 and leads to the root, through a scalar approach. The 3 is less stable than the root or 5, and starting on the 3 and walking down to the root is a nice color for your line.

FIG. 4.8. 12-Bar Blues Example 3. An asterisk (∗) indicates a non-root on beat 1.

Repeating the note in bar 1 is a way to add tension or suspense, and it adds some drama to the line, which then starts moving. Bar 2, beat 1 has the 5, which then walks up to the root on beat 4. Notice that we use the A natural. The A♭ is a chord tone, but the A natural is a much stronger way to move to the root. The A natural doesn't work well with the B♭ chord, and if this was a slow ballad, it would last too long. But in a walking line like this, it works well, as it adds motion towards the root. It is also diatonic to the key of F.

In bar 8, the D on beat 1 may look and sound a little unstable, but notice that it is really outlining the D7 chord that leads to the Gmi7, functioning as its secondary dominant (V7 of II).

FIG. 4.9. 12-Bar Blues Example 4. An asterisk indicates a non-root on beat 1.

61   62
Full Band   Play-Along

This line is a simple usage of roots and 5's, with chord tones and scale tones added for motion.

FIG. 4.10. 12-Bar Blues with Scale Tones

This example starts with a two feel, with some added notes for rhythmic interest. It eventually moves into a walk at bar 7, which is another way to add some interest or drama in your lines.

FIG. 4.11. Two Feel Then Walk

Rhythmic embellishment adds rhythmic interest and direction. Jazz eighth notes are sometimes notated as a dotted eighth followed by a sixteenth. They are usually felt as an eighth-note triplet figure with a tie between the first two eighths. Play this line with a jazz eighth-note feel.

FIG. 4.12. Jazz Eighths Written as Dotted Eighth/Sixteenths

Consider the harmonic and rhythmic directions of your line. The harmonic
direction is how one chord resolves to another. The rhythmic direction is the
feeling of drive and excitement—even if the line is just quarter notes. Later, we
will practice some syncopated lines.

FIG. 4.13. Harmonic and Rhythmic Direction Example 1

This line includes some chord substitutions and passing tones.

FIG. 4.14. Harmonic and Rhythmic Direction Example 2

"Sky Groove"

Here's a root and fifth, straight-eighth bass line. Notice that there are no scale or chromatic passing tones. Try to spice it up with some scale and/or chromatic passing tones.

Root and 5th Bossa

FIG. 4.15. "Sky Groove"

"Discover a New Infant"

A tune in a minor key. Notice how the AABA form is notated.

FIG. 4.16. "Discover a New Infant"

Here's a cycle-V line that has an interesting harmonic direction. It's straightforward all quarter notes, but the harmony gives it a lot of shape.

FIG. 4.17. Cycle-V Line

G Blues

71   72
Full Band   Play-Along

Here are three examples of a basic G blues, but set three ways. Notice how the rhythmic concept really defines the line. Also, notice the different ways the forms are notated. The D.C. al Coda is used in this case because it is more of a turnaround to the top; the coda is the ending.

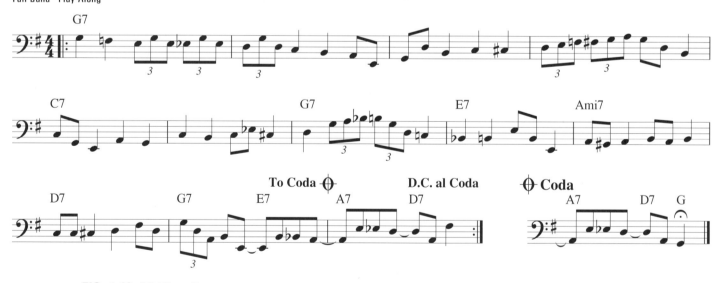

FIG. 4.18. "G Blues"

In this simplified line, the form is notated with a first and second ending.

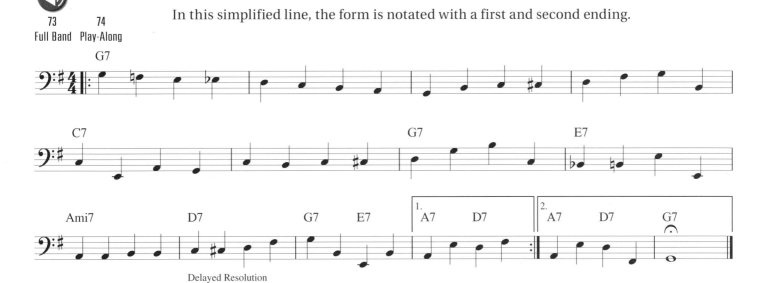

FIG. 4.19. G Blues Simplified

This third version adds just a little embellishment. The form is notated in a typical jazz style, with just a repeat bar. It is understood that you will either end on the G7 in bar 11 or continue with the turnaround, depending on whether you are ending the tune or not.

FIG. 4.20. G Blues with Embellishments

"Double Trouble"

"Double Trouble" doubles the notes. It was not unusual for early swing bass players (such as Walter Page, playing with Count Basie) to play double notes, which really provided the important feel that would make people dance. In addition, at fast tempos, double notes can help with the articulation and shape of a line. For another example, check out Charlie Haden playing with Ornette Coleman in the 1960s.

77   78
Full Band   Play-Along

FIG. 4.21. "Double Trouble"

CYCLE V COMMON CHORD PROGRESSION DRILL

Here are a number of different ways to play the common two-bar chord progression: IImi7 V7 IMaj7 VI7. Try mixing and matching the measures from each two-bar phrase. Always play the measures in sequence, although you can switch any measures 1 and 3 or any measures 2 and 4. Notice that the harmonic rhythm is two chords per measure.

79

FIG. 4.22. Cycle V Chord Progression

Here is a similar example. Notice that the harmonic rhythm is one chord per measure, whereas the previous one was two chords per measure. Also notice that the IIImi is substituting for the I major chord.

FIG. 4.23. Harmonic Phrases

HARMONIC LOOPS: ROOT MOTION OF MINOR THIRDS AND HALF-STEPS

This is a common post-bop progression. Practice these loops at many different tempos. Try setting a metronome on beats 2 and 4. It is a more sophisticated line.

FIG. 4.24. Harmonic Loops

CHAPTER 5

Ornaments, Articulations, and Rhythmic Embellishments

PULL-OFFS, DROPS, RAKES

Rakes, drops, skips, ghost notes, pull-offs (P.O.), and hammer-ons (H.O.) can be used to add rhythmic embellishment and movement/direction to a line.

These exercises demonstrate rakes across multiple strings. Rakes can be articulated in different ways, from ringing open strings (o), particularly at slower tempos, to dead-note articulations (x). Here, we'll use pizzicato open strings as indicated (o).

FIG. 5.1. Open Strings

In these next exercises, the numerals indicate plucking fingers. You will often move from your second (2) finger to your first (1), though not always. When the last note is the very lowest string, notice that you use the same finger for all the strings. If the last note is something other than the lowest string, then you use another finger. A good place to start is to pluck across the G, D, and A strings, which gives you the eighth-note triplet rhythm.

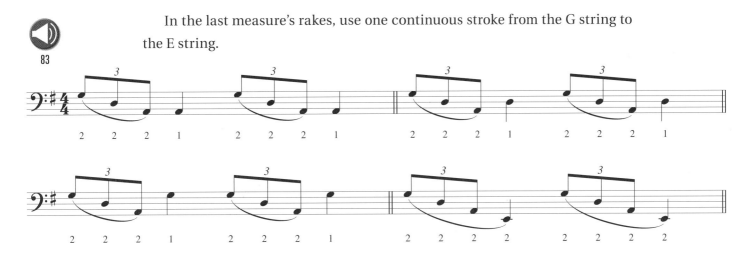

In the last measure's rakes, use one continuous stroke from the G string to the E string.

FIG. 5.2. Right-Hand Exercise 1

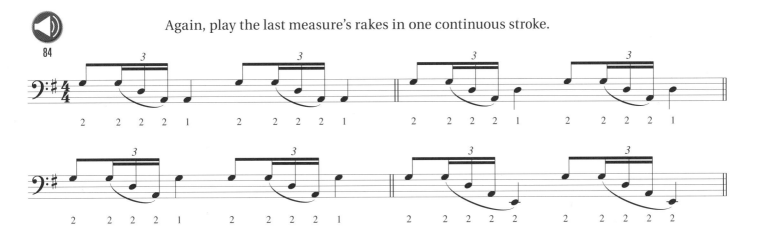

Again, play the last measure's rakes in one continuous stroke.

FIG. 5.3. Right-Hand Exercise 2

This type of rake is sometimes called a *rhythmic drop*, which is a rake that descends to a target note. Notice that they can be played from an octave root to the root, the 9 to the root, or the 7 to the root.

FIG. 5.4. Rhythmic Drop from 7 to Root

The "x" notes are "ghost" notes (sometimes called "dead" notes) played by muting the string with the fingerboard hand. This is achieved by lightly releasing the pressure on your fingerboard hand to produce a note that has more of a percussive sound than a defined pitch, though be aware that it may also produce harmonics.

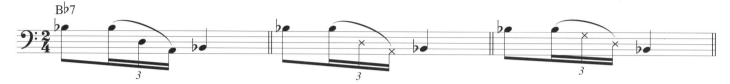

FIG. 5.5. Ghost Notes

Here is a short bass line using ghost-note drops. Practice these rhythmic drops from the 9 to the root, incorporating ghost notes.

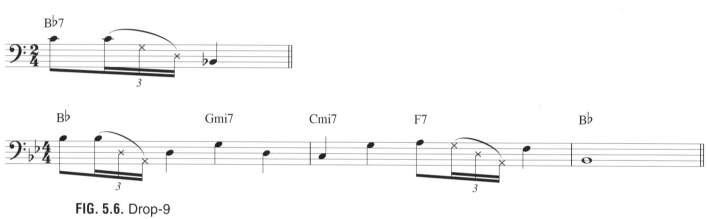

FIG. 5.6. Drop-9

RHYTHMIC EMBELLISHMENTS

The great drummer Papa Jo Jones would tell bass players he wanted "four on the floor" to match his bass drum (all quarter notes). In contemporary jazz, it is now more common for us to add or use some of these rhythmic embellishments. Be careful not to overuse them.

The jazz eighth note is the overriding feel of jazz, and must be considered when adding these ornaments or articulations. They come from the drummer's ride cymbal and snare fills, the melody, and many other sources. It gives rhythmic direction to the bass line.

Here are some examples of rhythmic embellishments you can add to a four-feel line. Try incorporating these rhythms into your bass lines.

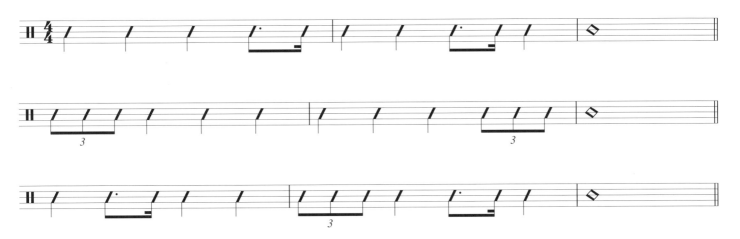

FIG. 5.7. Rhythmic Embellishments

88

Start with a simple jazz swing feel, like that of a drummer's ride cymbal. Play the following three exercises individually with repeats, or continue from one to the next without stopping. The next two figures are recorded back to back.

FIG. 5.8. Rhythmic Embellishment Example 1

Next, add some triplets.

FIG. 5.9. Rhythmic Embellishment Example 2

Notice how we have added a lot more activity in this example.

FIG. 5.10. Rhythmic Embellishment Example 3

Add more "rakes" and "drops," plus some dead notes and pull-offs. Notice measure 11, where the x notehead (G) is played as a pull-off with your fingerboard finger. It is characteristic to use open strings for pull-offs, but any note may be used.

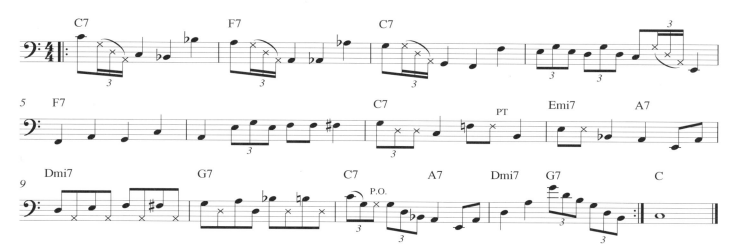

FIG. 5.11. Rhythmic Embellishment Example 4

At some point, the embellishments will become overbearing, so you will need to relax with some straight ahead quarter notes to settle everything down and be able to start building the intensity over again.

FIG. 5.12. Rhythmic Embellishment Example 5

HAMMER-ON

When you hammer on (H.O.) a string, your fingerboard hand produces the sound. Do not pluck the string with your other hand.

FIG. 5.13. Hammer-On

CHAPTER 6

Vamps, Pedal Points, Grooves, and Feels

You must be able to lay down a groove. Your attitude is also important. Make friends with all musicians, especially drummers; if you play well, they will help you get gigs. But you also have to be able to fulfill your primary function as a bass player, of laying down the groove—playing the foundation notes of the rhythm section, rather than soloing all the time, like you're a guitar player.

Play "bass bass," and make them dance. That's how to make the phone ring.

Vamps and *ostinatos* are a must for all bassists. They must be performed consistently for long periods of time and with a solid, hypnotic groove. You need to be able to play them without variation, without getting bored or sounding boring. And you need to be able to add a little tasteful spice, but without losing the groove flavor. This requires stamina and technique.

Pedal Point is another type of groove that is used in jazz bass playing.

In this chapter, we will explore these different types of bass grooves.

VAMPS

A "vamp" is a repetitive figure or groove, like an "ostinato," but for a rhythm section.

Have fun playing these vamps. Concentrate on your sound, time, and articulation. Practice them in different styles, tempos, and keys.

"Leave Your Boots at the Door"

Here's a well-known vamp in 6/8.

89 90
Full Band Play-Along

FIG. 6.1. "Leave Your Boots at the Door"

"Lethal José"

91   92
Full Band   Play-Along

This bass vamp has been used as an introduction to a song, as well as for the A section.

FIG. 6.2. "Lethal José"

"Totally Azure"

93   94
Full Band   Play-Along

"Totally Azure" can be played or felt in 6, 3, 12, or 4. Think about it.

FIG. 6.3. "Totally Azure"

"1, 5, 9"

95   96
Full Band   Play-Along

This vamp has a Latin feel. Try it in a fast "2" feel, also.

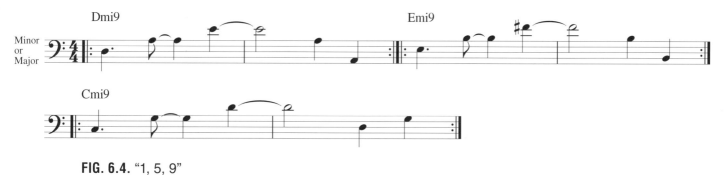

FIG. 6.4. "1, 5, 9"

"Rural Tune"

97   98
Full Band Play-Along
Double stops sound great on the bass.

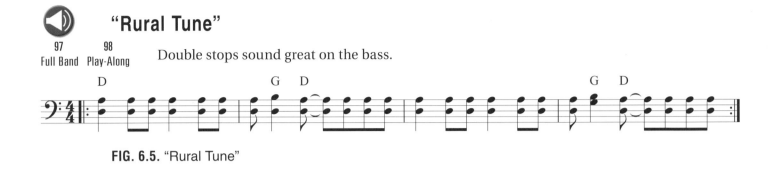

FIG. 6.5. "Rural Tune"

"Here's to Dad"

99   100
Full Band Play-Along
Here's a simple-but-catchy vamp that makes great use of just roots and 5's.

FIG. 6.6. "Here's to Dad"

VAMPS IN DIFFERENT METERS

Practice these vamps, which are in a variety of meters. Play each one four times.

101   102
Full Band Play-Along

103   104
Full Band Play-Along

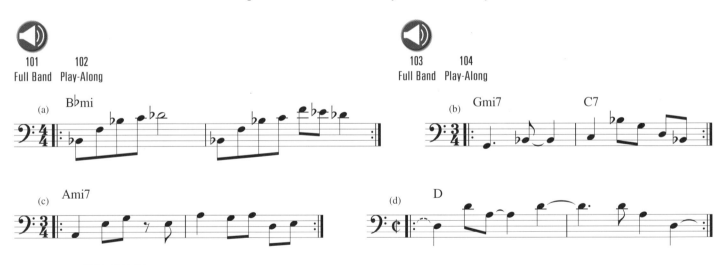

FIG. 6.7. Vamps

Practice these vamps in 6/8, which is a very interesting meter and can be approached many different ways. Practice each one over and over until it feels comfortable. Try them in different styles, tempos, and keys, and add different articulations.

FIG. 6.8. Vamps in 6/8

"Funky Bop"

A good exercise is to take a repetitive rhythm and see how many ways you can play it. On the vamps we've been playing, it's the same notes and rhythms, repeating over and over. Now, it's just the rhythm that repeats, but with different notes.

FIG. 6.9. "Funky Bop"

Try these vamp variations on a 5/4 groove.

FIG. 6.10. 5/4 Vamps

This 9/4 groove is like putting two measures of 4/4 together with a rest in the middle.

Swing/Funk

FIG. 6.11. Bass Rhumba in 9/4

PEDAL POINT

When a bass note is repeated under changing chords, it is called a "pedal point." In figure 6.12, the desired pedal tone is indicated below the staff, as well as notated. Play the notated examples first, and then experiment with pedals using your own ideas.

Pedal Point Exercises

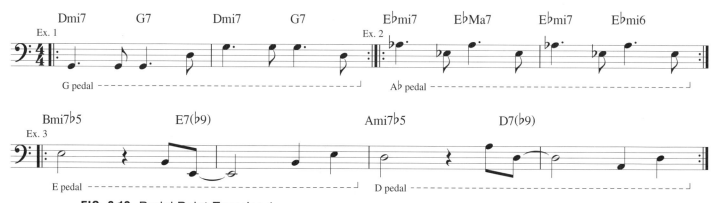

FIG. 6.12. Pedal Point Exercise 1

Play the twelve-bar (G) blues progression below, pedaling the tonic (G) for twelve bars, then pedal the dominant (D) for the next twelve bars.

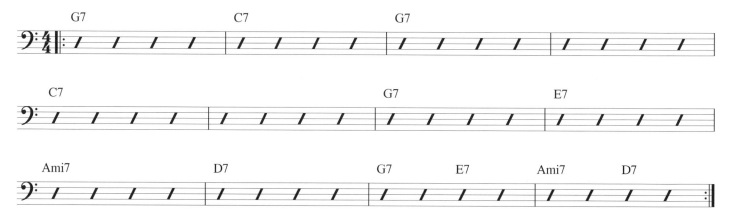

FIG. 6.13. Pedal Point Exercise 2

"On Verdant Flipper Avenue"

This is a good example of pedal point. On the recording, we play the tune using a pedal point on the A section. Then it swings on the B section. We do a chorus of improvisation where we walk. Then, we go back to the pedal point at the head and take the coda.

105 106
Full Band Play-Along

FIG. 6.14. "On Verdant Flipper Avenue"

"Many Evening Eyes"

Notice that in "Many Evening Eyes," we vary between a pedal point and walking bass in the different sections. Pedal points provide opportunities to be creative rhythmically while emphasizing one note.

Pedal point gives you a great opportunity to explore "broken time." *Broken time* is a style in jazz where the rhythm is strong, but not stated in the usual walking style; rather, it is more syncopated. Using space and playing notes across the bar line are two of the common ways to play broken time. You almost pretend that you are not playing time, but you actually know where it is. The time is still happening, but it is happening inside you. You are breaking the time up so that it is less obvious. The early ECM records featured a lot of this style of playing.

Being able to play broken time well requires a stronger sense of groove, because it is not stated. You really need to have the groove in your body, even though you are not playing it.

The example below is based on the chords to a popular jazz standard. Play the pedal broken and walk on the rest of the piece.

This tune uses pedal point, it moves between a straight eighth and walking feel, and also broken time.

107   108
Full Band   Play-Along

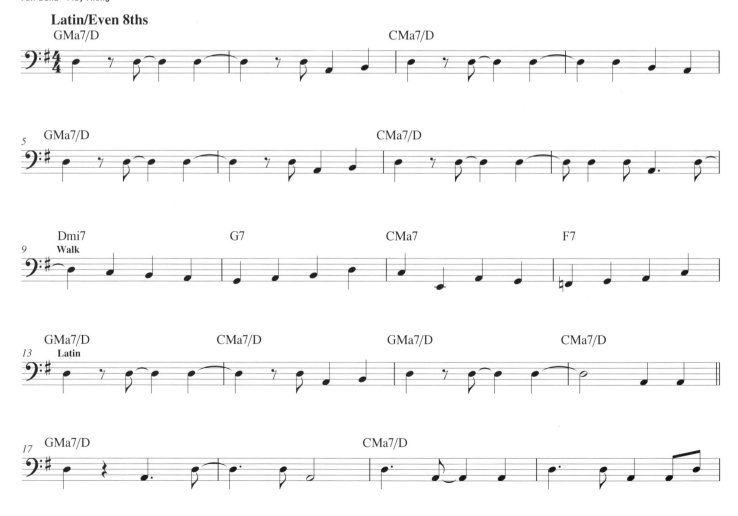

FIG 6.15. "Many Evening Eyes" with Pedal Point and Broken Time

GROOVES

Another part of jazz players' time concept, which ties into vamps and ostinatos, is "groove playing."

Strictly repetitive vamps and ostinatos can be a useful type of bass line. The idea of repeating bass figures, though, can be expanded and applied more generally into groove playing. To "play a groove" means that you are focused on setting up a solid foundation for the rest of the band, with a consistent, repetitive, solid bass part. This is in comparison with more melodic playing styles, like what you might find in melodically intricate or through-composed styles of playing.

Here's a common quarter-note bass line. Notice how we can vary it to create many different grooves. Having a comprehensive groove vocabulary is important for any bass player.

FIG. 6.16. Rhythmic Variation Example 1

Adding some space can help your groove breathe. Practice these variations of the funk line from the previous exercise, but now with additional space and syncopation.

FIG. 6.17. Rhythmic Variation Example 2

New Orleans Style "Second Line" Groove

109 110
Full Band Play-Along

In New Orleans, when bands march down the street, the horns are usually walking first, and then the rhythm section is the second line.

FIG. 6.18. New Orleans Groove Example 1

111 112
Full Band Play-Along

FIG. 6.19. New Orleans Groove Example 2

FIG. 6.20. New Orleans Groove Example 3

FIG. 6.21. New Orleans Groove Example 4

FIG. 6.22. Bass Rhumba Example 2

FIG. 6.23. Heavy Backbeat

12/8 Grooves

The 12/8 meter is a triplet subdivision of 4/4, and it is a very important feel for many styles: jazz, shuffle blues, and others. Here are some examples.

Dead Notes
Left Hand Mutes

FIG. 6.24. Vamp Example 1

FIG. 6.25. Vamp Example 2

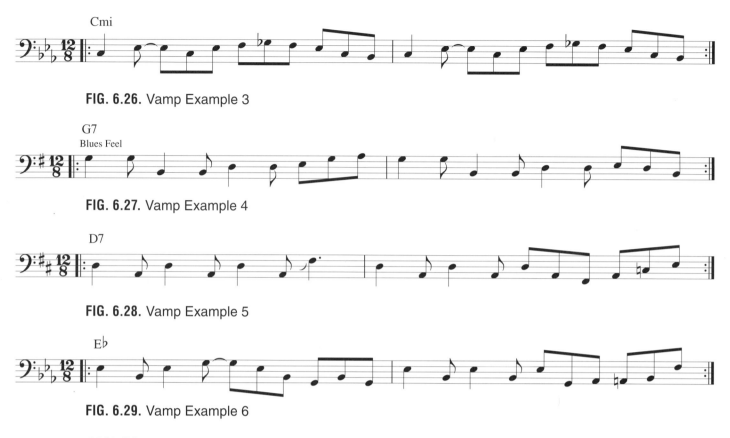

FIG. 6.26. Vamp Example 3

FIG. 6.27. Vamp Example 4

FIG. 6.28. Vamp Example 5

FIG. 6.29. Vamp Example 6

12/8 Blues

Here are some blues progressions using the 12/8 groove. Remember, the 12/8 feel uses triplet subdivision in the count as opposed to the duple subdivision of 4/4. 12/8 still counts as four beats to the measure, but the feel is the triplet. If you were dancing, very often, you'd be dancing in 4/4, but it's really 12/8; you are feeling the triplets on each beat.

Notice the phrasing marks in bar 9, sometimes used in 12/8 to reinforce the triplet feel. If you see that, you should interpret it as a slur, not a tie; play the eighth note legato. It's like a horn player playing "tenuto," or only lightly tongued/rearticulated.

119   120
Full Band Play-Along

FIG. 6.30. Shuffle Blues

FIG. 6.31. Triplet Feel

Variation, somewhat simpler:

FIG. 6.32. Triplet Feel with Rhythmic Variation

"Hot Season"

Here's a great minor song using the 12/8 feel. Notice the over-arching rhythm played by the drums and bass, anticipating the second beat.

FIG. 6.33. "Hot Season" Rhythm

123
Full Band

124
Play-Along

FIG. 6.34. "Hot Season"

It's not unusual to write a 12/8 feel in 4/4. So, here's the second chorus, now written in 4/4. Notice the use of all the triplets to reinforce the 12/8 feel.

FIG. 6.35. "Hot Season" Walk

"Mail Order Amour"

It is also not uncommon to count or feel 12/8 in 4/4. Just lock into a triplet on each quarter note in 4/4.

FIG. 6.36. "Mail Order Amour"

"Anticipation at the Photo Store"

Here are two types of grooves used in jazz waltz: a one feel and a two-against-three feel. A waltz is felt in "one." This means that there is primarily one important beat in the measure. In a two-against-three feel, you are putting two strong pulses in three beats, which creates tension. You are taking the six eighth notes, and tying three together, so that you are hitting the downbeat of 1 and the upbeat before beat 3.

FIG. 6.37. Two-Against-Three

Here is a jazz waltz using a "one" feel in the first eight bars and a two-against-three feel in sections of the second eight bars. Check out the form (ABAC) of this classic set of changes. We must be the keepers of the form.

129   130
Full Band   Play-Along

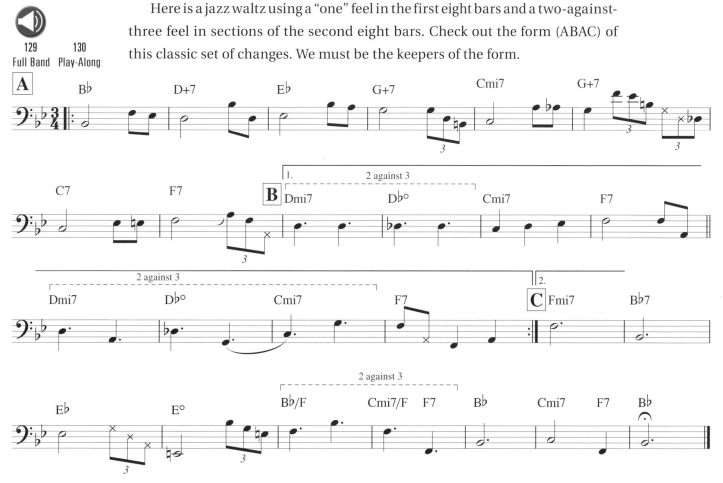

FIG. 6.38. "Anticipation at the Photo Store"

LISTENING LIST

- "Footprints," Miles Davis
- "All Blues," Miles Davis
- "Song for My Father," Horace Silver
- "Chameleon," Herbie Hancock

CHAPTER 7

Solo Playing

Jazz bass playing has made enormous strides in the past hundred years. Even though many jazz bassists will tell you that soloing is "icing on the cake," it is a must for today's contemporary player.

Throughout this book is a blend of our three different styles of playing and teaching. We present many of the gems we have discovered for soloing, in this chapter, in hopes that some will appeal to you and help you to develop your own distinct style.

HAND POSITION AND SOLOING

In this chapter, we'll talk about two types of soloing: bass-line and melodic soloing (which is more hornlike/vocal). With bass-line soloing, your right-hand technique will be the same as if you're playing bass lines.

For melodic soloing, in order to have more control over speed and articulation, you may want to use more than one finger, and bring the angle of your hand up across the strings—perpendicular to the strings, rather than parallel. It's not unusual for bass players to use a blend of the two. What matters most is the sound.

An important thing that can help in this area is to watch your favorite players perform and to watch yourself perform, in a mirror. By watching your favorite players and yourself play, you can bring the concept of their approach into your own playing.

This isn't a book about technique, and there are many ways to be successful in playing the bass. Here are some photos of all three of us authors and the various ways that we play.

Acoustic

(a) One-finger pluck at the end of the fingerboard, à la Ray Brown, for a strong, clean, clear sound

(b) Two-finger pluck, low on the fingerboard

(c) Similar to (b), but with more open fingers, good for a fast walk or for soloing

(d) Bruce Gertz demonstrating upright left-hand technique

(e) Left-hand double stop

Electric

(f) Rich Appleman demonstrating an upright-bass style pluck on a 5-string electric

(g) Upright style pluck, dampening with the thumb, good for walking bass

(h) Left hand on the fingerboard

(i) One-finger pluck, dampening
with the thumb

(j) Whit Browne on electric

(k and l) Left-hand double stops

FIG. 7.1. Hand Positions

BASS-LINE SOLOS

Building a solo that also keeps the integrity of a walking line is a good way to keep both the time and the form intact. Bass-line soloing is an older concept, but still very effective and can be both challenging and creative.

Originally, a bass-line solo meant that everyone else would lay out and the bass player would just continue with his walking line. Bands like "The Red Hot Peppers" (Jelly Roll Morton's band) might have an eight-bar bass-line solo at the end. Bass-line soloing can include pizzicato, arco, and/or slap playing. Eventually, as jazz moved from swing to bebop, and the emphasis was more on improvisation, the bass player began playing more vocal/melodic solos. Jimmy Blanton is considered the father of modern bass playing, and played in the swing period. Oscar Pettiford is the father of bebop bass playing. Listen to him playing on recordings such as "The Man I Love" (Coleman Hawkins' band) where you can hear him breathing. This shows how he was really thinking about vocal lines, as opposed to earlier solos that were mostly based on quarter notes.

Here is an example of a walking bass-line solo.

"Indiana Lee"

131   132
Full Band   Play-Along

FIG. 7.2. "Indiana Lee"

"Hot Home"

This walking bass solo is truly melodic, and there are almost no roots on the downbeats of the changes. It is a good improvisation study; however, it is not intended as an accompaniment.

To perform this tune, use this approach for the arrangement.

1. Chorus 1: Play in two.

2. Chorus 2: Walk.

3. Chorus 3: Play the written walking solo in figure 7.3.

4. Chorus 4: Improvise in a melodic style.

FIG. 7.3. "Hot Home" Walking Solo

SYMMETRICAL DIMINISHED SCALE

In the "Hot Home" solo, the chord scales used are the half-step/whole-step *symmetrical diminished* scales, which alternate half steps and whole steps. Listen to the improvised bass line on track 135, and then practice this notated walking line with track 136. Then improvise your own walking line using the same techniques.

FIG. 7.4. Symmetrical Diminished Scales

"Important Events"

In this solo, four-bar phrases are useful for motivic development and form integrity. Remember that a jazz bassist is a musical architect who must build and shape a line that supports the music.

Some might think that playing on two chords is easy or boring. The written line in figure 7.5 is a good example of creative use of minor scales. The recorded solo is another creative solo over these extended harmonic regions. Pay attention to the different techniques used, and think about how you might perform over these changes.

135   136
Full Band Play-Along

FIG. 7.5. "Important Events"

Developing a One-Chord Modal Walking Line

Here is another solo based on just two chords. As you practice it, notice the different melodic development techniques in use.

FIG. 7.6. "Important Events" Walking Modal Line

MELODIC SOLOS

In most jazz settings, the bass solo represents a sudden sonic change in the music that requires preparation. Good jazz bassists develop a "Jekyll and Hyde" concept of being able to play strong supportive "money notes" and then becoming melodic singers on their instruments.

Melodic solos require additional skill and practice, beyond solos that are more closely tied to bass lines. Melodic solos often make use of the bass's upper range. These lines may be rhythmically active, and often incorporate fragments of the tune's melody.

Many bassists transcribe certain horn players, especially Chet Baker and Miles Davis, for melodic soloing ideas that work well on bass. Don't forget to breathe.

The solo ideas will require a greater knowledge of modes and scales, and a good, solid sound, to keep the listeners' attention.

When a bass player solos, sometimes, the piano player and drummer will feed you ideas. Sometimes, the other musicians just stop. So, soloing requires an awareness of what the band is doing.

Melodic solos can feature runs—usually rising and/or falling scales, arpeggios, or chromatic lines—which are often played as fills.

Here are some options about how to choose notes for a melodic solo.

Vertical

137 138
Full Band Play-Along

Improvising can include running the chord arpeggios up and down. We call this "vertical" playing. Here is an example of vertical playing, from chord arpeggios.

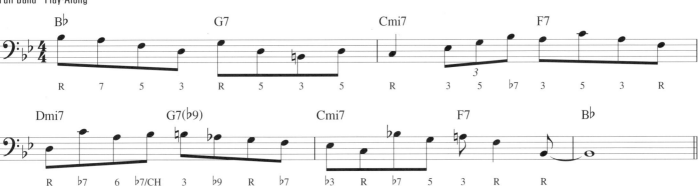

FIG. 7.7. Vertical Solo Playing

Horizontal

Another approach is "linear" or "horizontal" playing. In this approach, you play more melodically over the chords, usually in a diatonic key related progression. Similarly, you might play from the scale of the keys of the progression or play off the actual melody notes.

Figure 7.8 shows horizontal/linear playing. Here, we play from the key area of B♭, using the B♭ blues scale or B♭ Mixolydian with chromatic approach tones. Also think of "common tones"—notes that can be played over different chords. The notes are from the key of the moment or scale that fits over the diatonic four-bar phrase.

139   140
Full Band   Play-Along

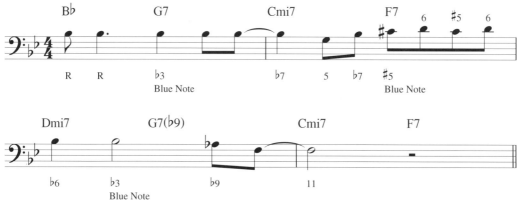

FIG. 7.8. Horizontal Solo Playing

RHYTHMIC ARTICULATIONS

Because the bass is in a low register, it is especially important to articulate your rhythms cleanly. To get your solo ideas across, you must have very clean articulation. Without that, your low notes won't be heard, and it won't be clear how they relate to the time.

The most important factor is the groove and phrasing of your solo. Remember that "jazz eighth notes" are actually played from a triplet feel rather than as "even" eighth notes.

Example:

FIG. 7.9. Jazz Eighths Written

This is actually felt like this:

FIG. 7.10. Jazz Eighths Felt

ARTICULATIONS

It is often possible to identify a great player by listening to them play just a couple notes, because of the way they articulate. Articulation is important to consider in your soloing. Remember the articulations we discussed in chapter 5. Here are some additional ones, especially useful in melodic soloing.

∧ = "Sting," like short accent but not a staccato note

> = Full value note accent

Similarly, syncopations add variety to a line, but to rhythm. Articulations can help to reinforce the freshness of the syncopated figure. Try these examples that use syncopation and articulation to add rhythmic variety to a swing eighth-note line.

FIG. 7.11. Syncopation

FIG. 7.12. Articulations

141
Full Band

142
Play-Along

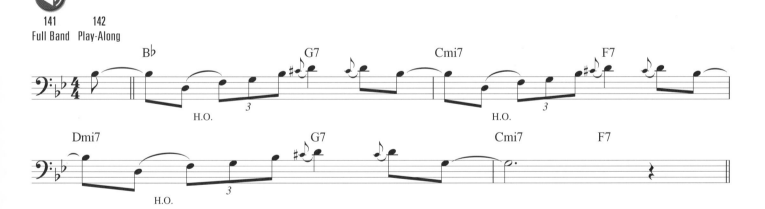

FIG. 7.13. Grace Notes

Remember, hammer-ons and pull-offs are done with your fingering hand and are widely used to create swing lines on a string instrument. We don't articulate every note, but we slur the hammer-ons (H.O.) and pull-offs (P.O.). The use of these articulations creates an unevenness that is characteristic of jazz phrasing. A classical player reading an eighth-note line will play them evenly, but a jazz player will have an unevenness that contributes to the swing feel. Swinging and walking are not marching; they are uneven feels.

BEBOP IDEAS FOR SOLOING

This "lick" is based on a "riff." A riff is a group of notes, usually a two-bar or four-bar phrase, that is repeated over the diatonic chord progression for the four-bar phrase and eight-bar phrase. (In a diatonic chord progression, all the chords are related to the key area. While there may be a chord tone or two outside the key, they are based all in the same key sound.)

Note: This chord progression comes from rhythm changes, but it uses a G7 instead of the original tune's G minor as the second chord of the progression. One of the things that came from bebop was "jazzing up the harmony." This G7 (V7 of II) became a common substitute chord, as it leads more easily into the II chord. This is a good example of how jazz musicians changed the harmony of the original tunes.

143   144
Full Band Play-Along

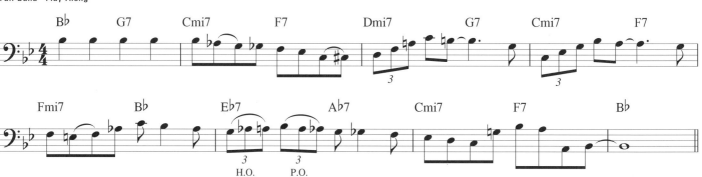

FIG. 7.14. Resolution

Another way to build a solo on these changes is by combining the relative minor and the blues scales.

FIG. 7.15. G Minor Scale and B♭ Blues Scale on B♭7

Here's that example in B♭ major, with a solo that is based more on G minor and G minor blues.

145   146
Full Band Play-Along

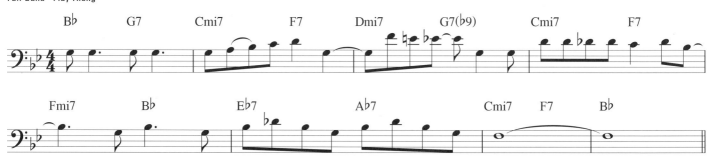

FIG. 7.16. B♭ Progression

Figure 7.17 has a four-bar continuous eighth-note phrase, followed by a call-and-response style phrase with more syncopation. Notice the rhythmic differences in these two four-bar phrases. They share similar shapes, both starting on mid-range B♭ and ending on a low-range B♭.

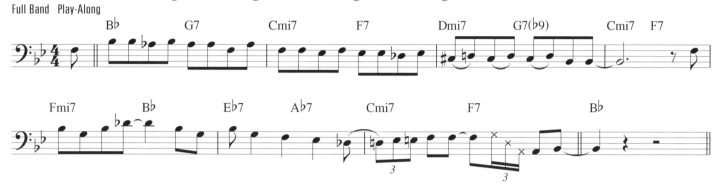

FIG. 7.17. Solo Playing

This phrase uses a B♭ diminished 7 arpeggio or B♭ symmetrical diminished scale (half step, whole step, etc.), and will give an "outside" sound of tension over the diatonic B♭ chord progression.

FIG. 7.18. Symmetrical Diminished Solo Playing

This solo has a feel of an embellished bass line solo, but it is more active and a little more melodic than standard bass lines. If it were a more melodic solo, it would have more breaths and syncopation. It is very much in the style of Ray Brown.

FIG. 7.19. Rhythm Changes

"Fall Foliage"

This exercise alternates between roots and melodic notes, and it is a good exercise for intonation and ear training. Using roots and guide tones (3's and 7's) can help you hear a tune or chord progression, and it can also give many ideas for improvising. Explore playing this using some harmonics. Let the first notes of each measure ring.

FIG. 7.20. "Fall Foliage"

"My Whole Life"

Here's a solo that incorporates a famous melody. Always consider the song melody in your soloing. Learning the words to the song also helps with the melody and its meaning, and helps you keep your place in the song. It's a great way to think about soloing.

In this example, the melody is incorporated into the solo using several different approaches.

1. Soloing off the melody, using its fragments in other ideas

2. Reinterpreting the original, changing its notes and rhythms

3. Bringing the melody line into a solo, quoting it verbatim

FIG. 7.21. "My Whole Life"

Phrase Variations

Here are two more active variations of the first eight bars of the song. While the original uses the melody, these variations get further away from it. While you play the variations, continue to keep the melody in your mind.

Variation 1

157   158
Full Band Play-Along

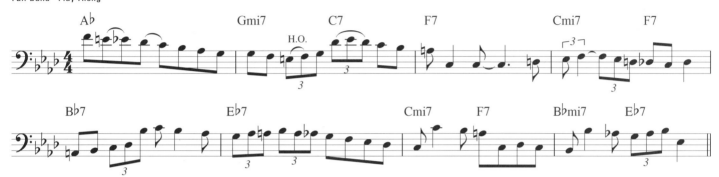

FIG. 7.22. "My Whole Life" Excerpt 1

Variation 2

159   160
Full Band Play-Along

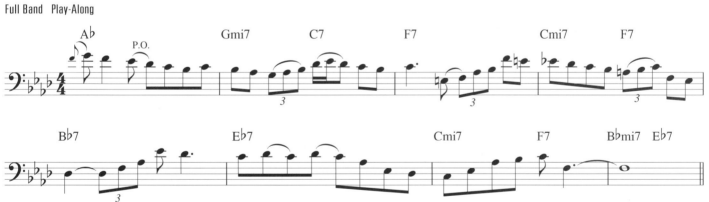

FIG. 7.23. "My Whole Life" Excerpt 2

"Thinking About Someone"

161   162
Full Band   Play-Along

Here's a solo on another jazz standard.

FIG. 7.24. "Thinking About Someone"

"Hot Season" Solo

163
Full Band

164
Play-Along

FIG. 7.25. "Hot Season" Solo

This is a challenging chord progression from the post bebop period.

165   166
Full Band   Play-Along

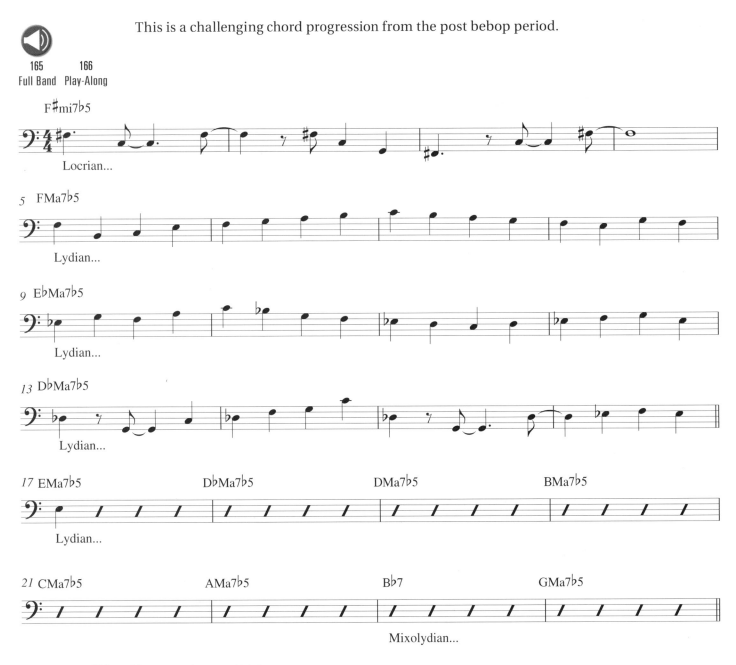

FIG. 7.26. "Wish from Within"

This variation of the last section of "Wish from Within" is an interesting use of all major 7 chords with one dominant 7. Many would call this a "constant structure" form, where you're using nearly all the same chord type. Use the Lydian mode on the major 7 chords.

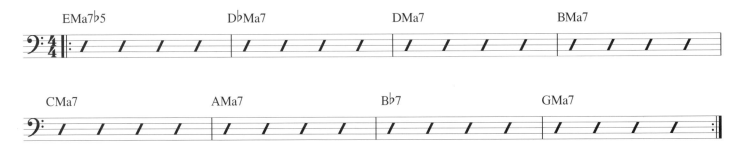

FIG. 7.27. "Wish from Within" Constant Structure

GUIDELINES FOR TRANSCRIBING

Transcribing is a way to develop vocabulary and get ideas for soloing.

Good jazz bass players must recognize chord types and hear chord changes. Remember that every new tune you learn is a new bass line. Try to hear "around the corner." After you've learned many songs, there are familiar chord progressions, and many of them are repeated. Try to anticipate the chord that is coming up. You might be surprised! But the fact that you anticipate the chord that will sound good is a great starting point. If the chord is a surprise, you'll be more likely to figure out what it should be.

Transcribing and call-and-response are useful tools in developing this ability to anticipate what will come next. Here are some guidelines to help you transcribe solos.

1. Listen for the key. (Bass usually plays roots.)

2. Sing and play the scale of that key.

3. Repeat a short phrase over and over, until you can sing in the key with it and eventually sing the phrase.

4. Count time while listening to the phrase again. Determine which beat (or "and" of a beat) it begins on and whether it includes eighth notes, quarter notes, rests, etc.

5. Subtleties will come after the basic music is written down. Always use pencil, as you'll probably need to change many notes and rhythms while zeroing in on the exact sound.

6. Be persistent. Don't be discouraged, even if it takes many repetitions to play seemingly simple passages perfectly. After some time, the task of transcribing becomes easier. You will begin recognizing both rhythmic and melodic passages similar to those you have already transcribed.

WHAT IS IMPROVISATION IN MUSIC?

As we learn to use our imagination and build stories in our minds, the same idea can evolve through music.

After learning a vocabulary for a language, people develop their own means of communication with that vocabulary. This might be called a style or even a concept, however it can vary to large degrees within these frames. People can be more or less dramatic when speaking, depending on the context. Dynamic levels and accented words or phrases can drastically alter how a person communicates both verbally and musically.

It is said that there are those who aspire to *reach boundaries* and those who *move the boundaries further*. The "stylist" could be described as a musician who is strictly and firmly a swing player—someone who stays within the boundaries of authentic-sounding swing music. There is nothing wrong with mastering an idiom or period of music, and it is important for many professional musicians to be able to play with stylistic authenticity. Sometimes, though, we want to break through the boundaries of specific styles and create something new. Some musicians break through boundaries and continue to extend them throughout their careers. John Coltrane, Charlie Parker, and Thelonious Monk come to mind as examples of artists moving boundaries, and bassists Ray Brown, Oscar Pettiford, Paul Chambers, and Charles Mingus as well. Some also refer to this as raising the bar.

Composers are improvisers in the sense that they form musical ideas from the same material that jazz musicians and composers use: rhythmic, melodic, and harmonic vocabulary. The improviser and composer both put their vocabulary to use while telling their stories through music.

The development of our inner ear and musical receptors is a very essential goal for those aspiring to be improvisers and performers with other musicians. Practicing rhythmic, harmonic, and melodic phrasing, both diatonically and chromatically, will help develop skills. Listening and playing with other musicians is as important as practicing. The quicker your ears can decipher musical information, the better a communicator you'll become.

Improvisation is the ability to communicate with other musicians and audiences through use of musical *vocabulary* to tell a story as both an accompanist and/or a soloist.

Good News/Good News

Having completed this material (congrats), you are well on your way as a jazz bassist. Even though our combined years of performing, teaching, and studying jazz are equal to the history of jazz, we will never be finished. There will always be something new to listen to or play. Have fun.

—Bruce, Rich, Whit

ABOUT THE AUTHORS

Photo by Moti Hodis

Rich Appleman is chair emeritus of the bass department at Berklee College of Music, where he taught thousands of students over four decades. As a bassist, he performed or recorded with Lionel Hampton, Sweets Edison, Al Grey, Rosemary Clooney, Lin Biviano Big Band, the Fringe, the Boston Pops, the Jeff Covell Trio, Ryles Big Band, the Sandy Prager Trio, Gregory Hines, Bernadette Peters, Boston Musical Theater, and others. Rich performed in pit orchestras for shows such as *A Chorus Line, Cats, Les Misérables, 42nd Street,* and *Miss Saigon*. Rich is the author of three other books with Berklee Press: *Reading Contemporary Electric Bass, The Berklee Practice Method: Bass,* and *Chord Studies for Electric Bass*. He currently teaches bass through Berklee's online continuing education division.

Photo by Rich Appleman

Whit Browne, professor of bass, has been teaching at Berklee College of Music since 1976. Whit has been playing the bass since 1964. He has made many recordings and TV and radio appearances, and has performed with Oscar Peterson, Dizzy Gillespie, Diana Krall, Sonny Stitt, Eddie "Lockjaw" Davis, Kenny Burrell, Alan Dawson, Papa Jo Jones, Joe Williams, and many other jazz artists. Whit is listed in "15 Notable Arts Professors in Boston" 2014 by The Art Career, and received the "Outstanding Contribution to the Arts" award from Harvard University. Whit has been nominated three times for "Outstanding Bassist" by the Boston Music Awards, and received "Award for Excellence in Bass Instruction" from Berklee College of Music. He studied with Ray Brown, Charlie Banacos, Kai Juel, and Tiny Martin.

Photo by Jonathan Feist

Bruce Gertz is an award-winning bassist (acoustic and electric), composer, educator, and author. He is a professor of bass at Berklee College of Music, where he has taught since 1976.

Bruce is the recipient of National Endowment for the Arts Jazz Performance Award Grant, Massachusetts Cultural Council Musical Composition Award, and numerous awards for outstanding bassist, from Boston Music Awards, A.S.C.A.P. Plus Popular Awards, and multiple recognition awards from the International Association of Jazz Educators and the Jazz Education Network. Bruce also serves on the board of directors of the International Society of Bassists.

Bruce has performed and recorded with such artists as Gary Burton, Jerry Bergonzi, John Abercrombie, Joey Calderazzo, Kenny Werner, Mick Goodrick, Kurt Rosenwinkel, Billy Hart, George Garzone, Mike Stern, Larry Coryell, Joe Lovano, Cab Calloway, Count Basie, and many others.

His extensive discography and additional information can be found at www.openmindjazz.com/bruce-gertz.

INDEX